Insect coloring book

Published by Gizzy Books Ltd   2016

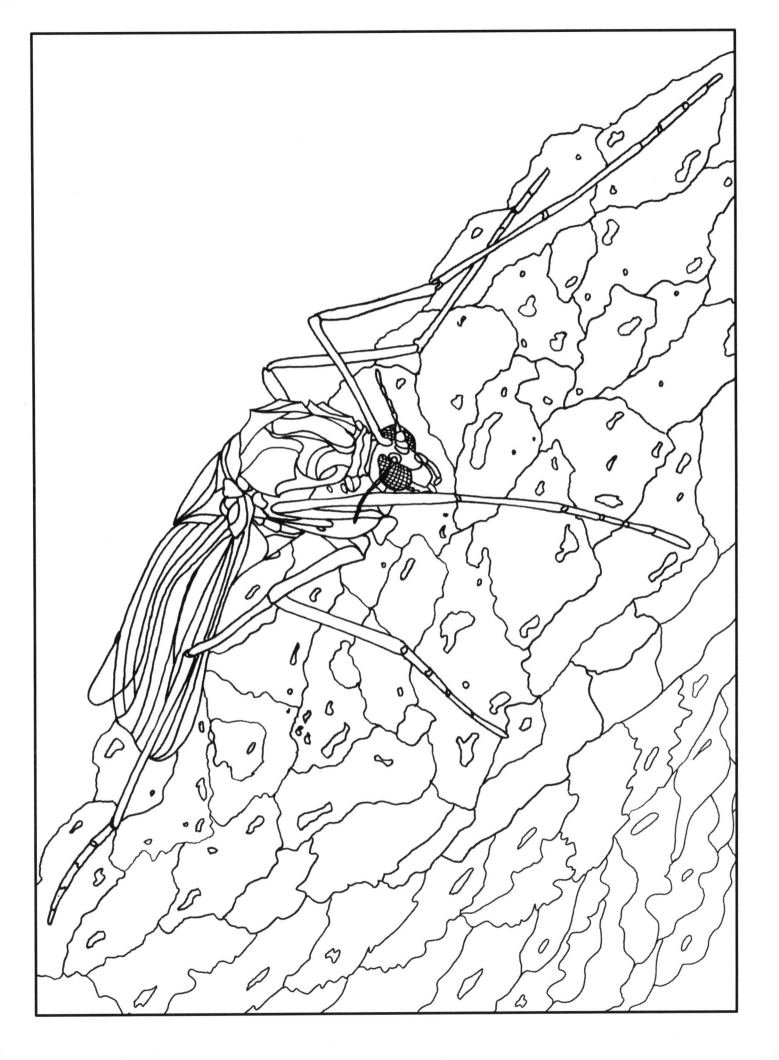

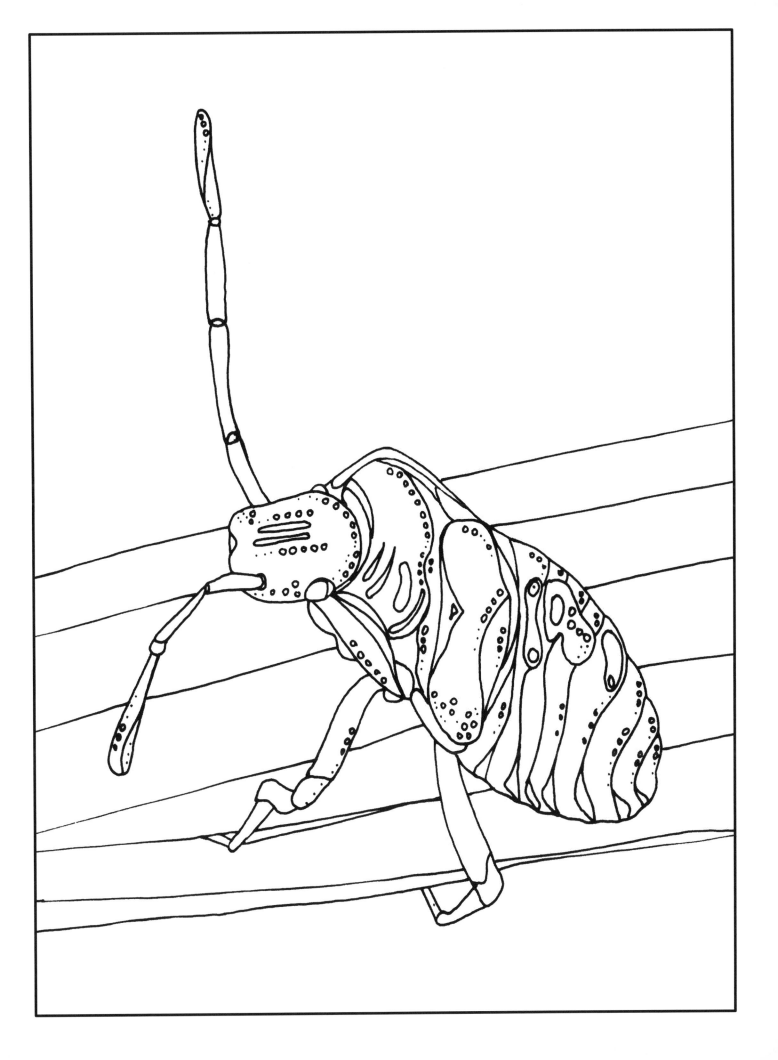

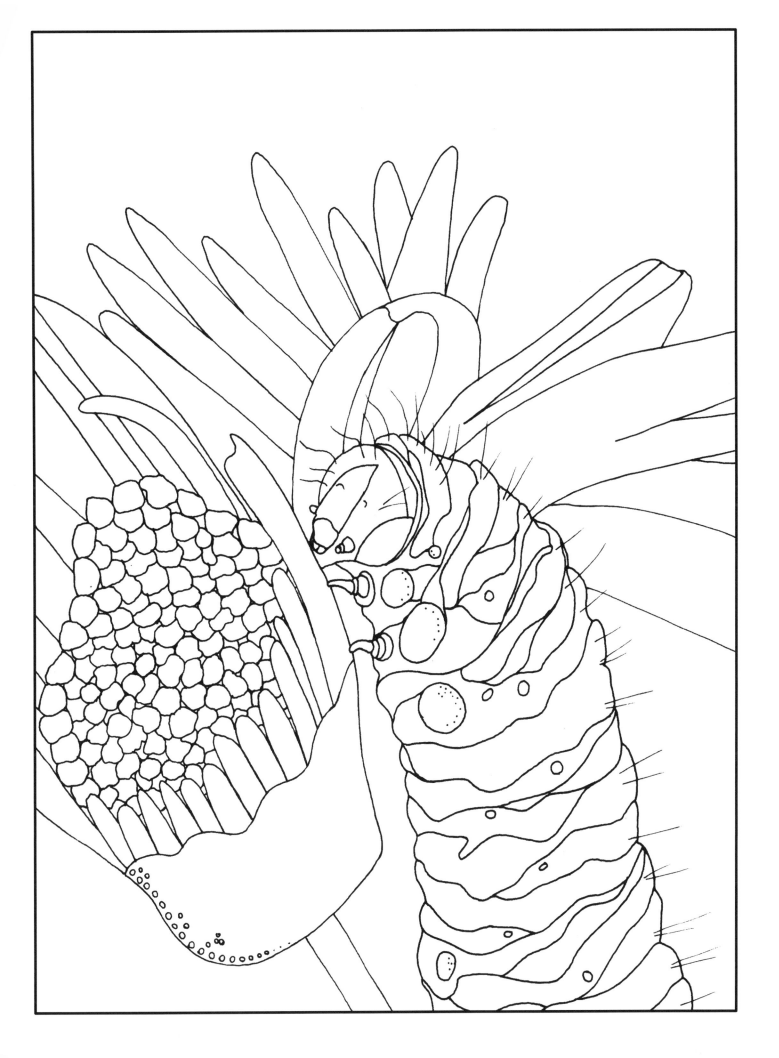

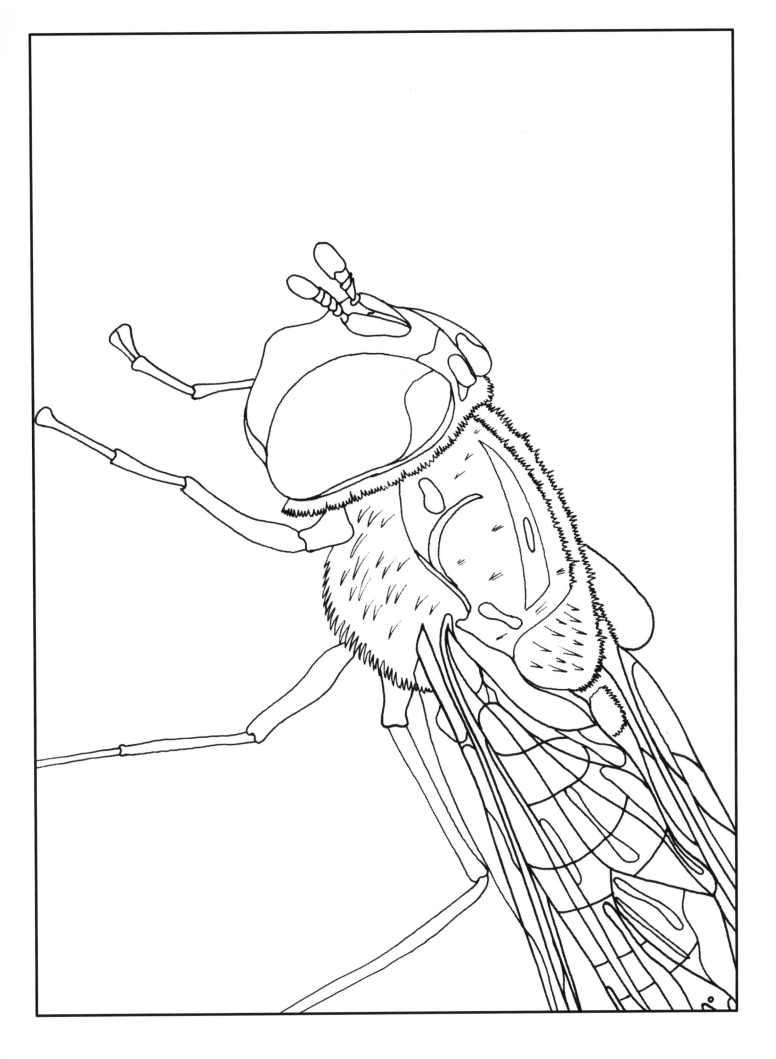

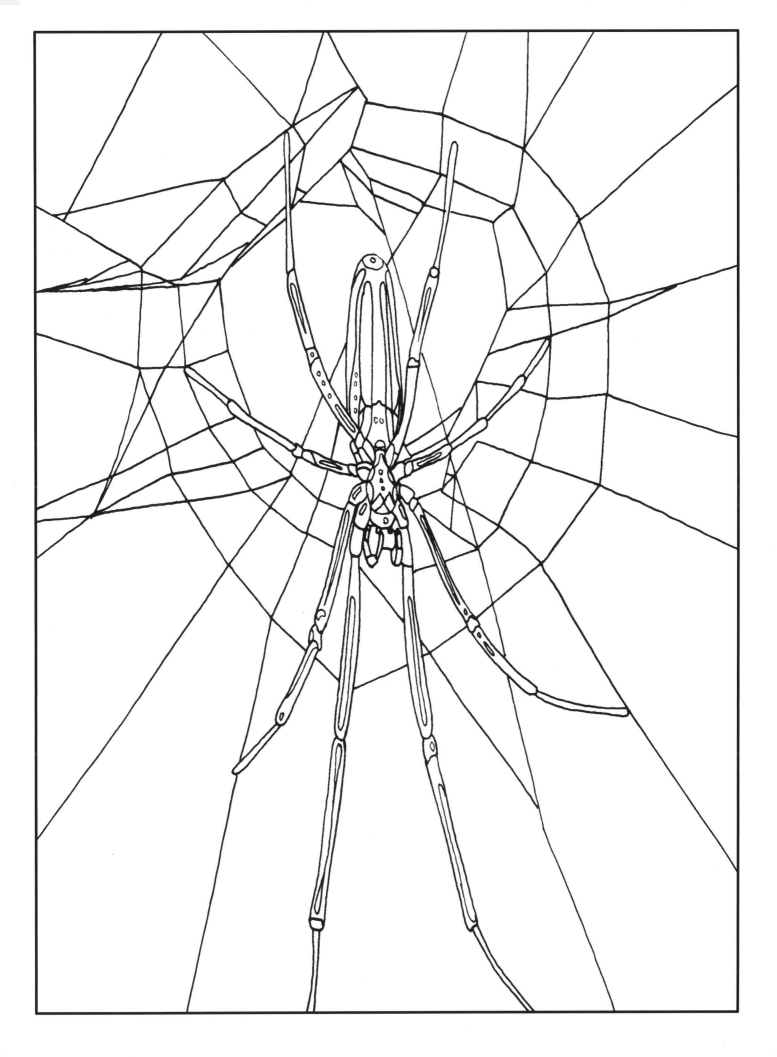

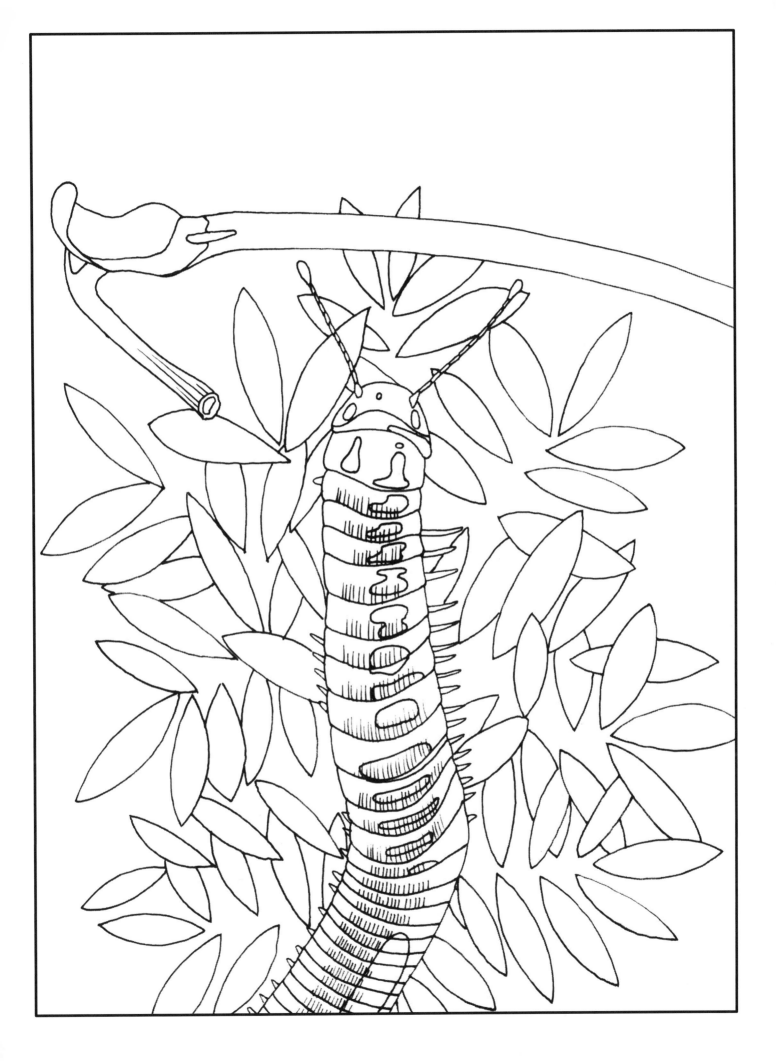

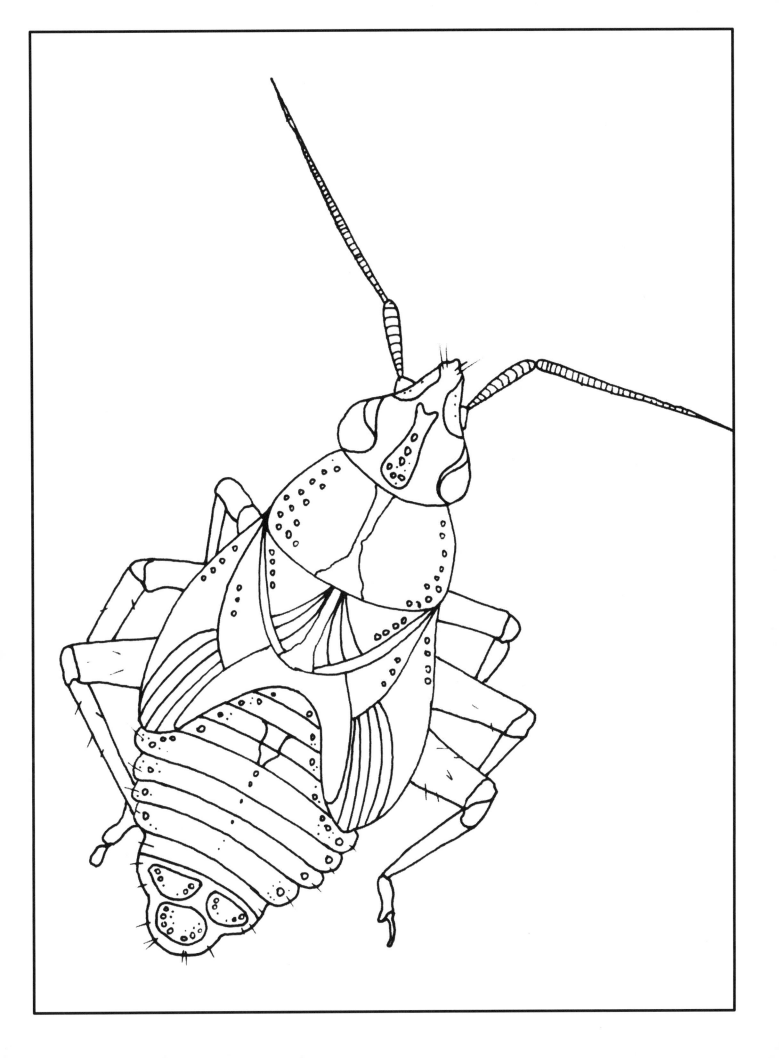

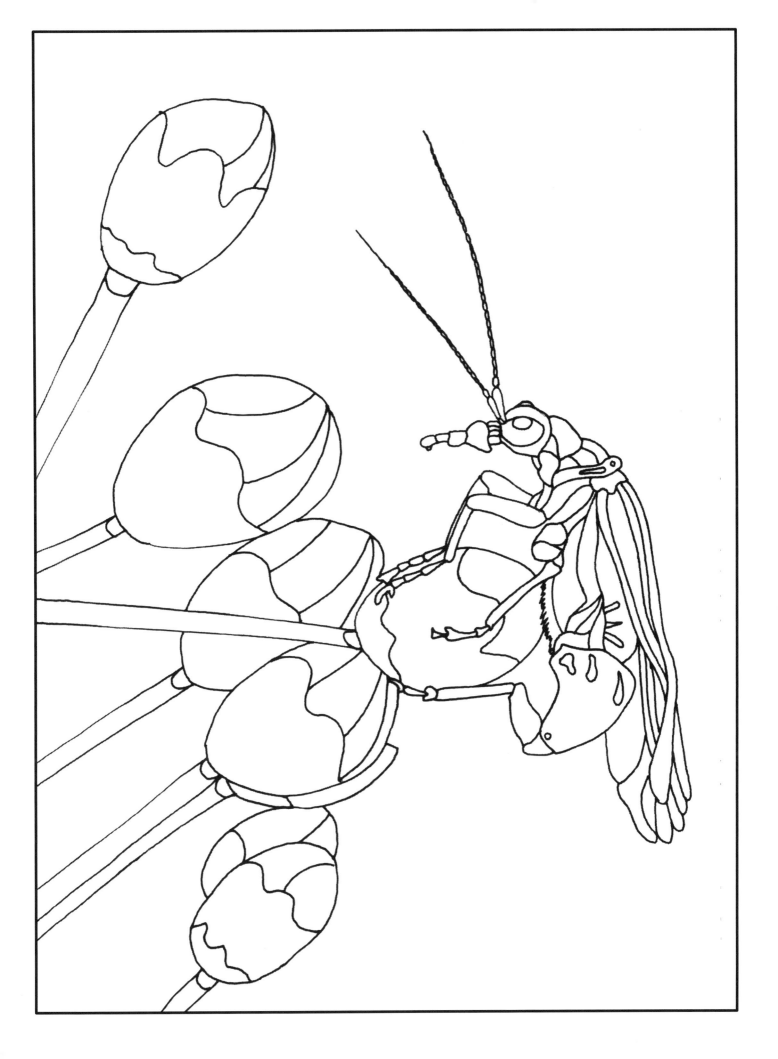

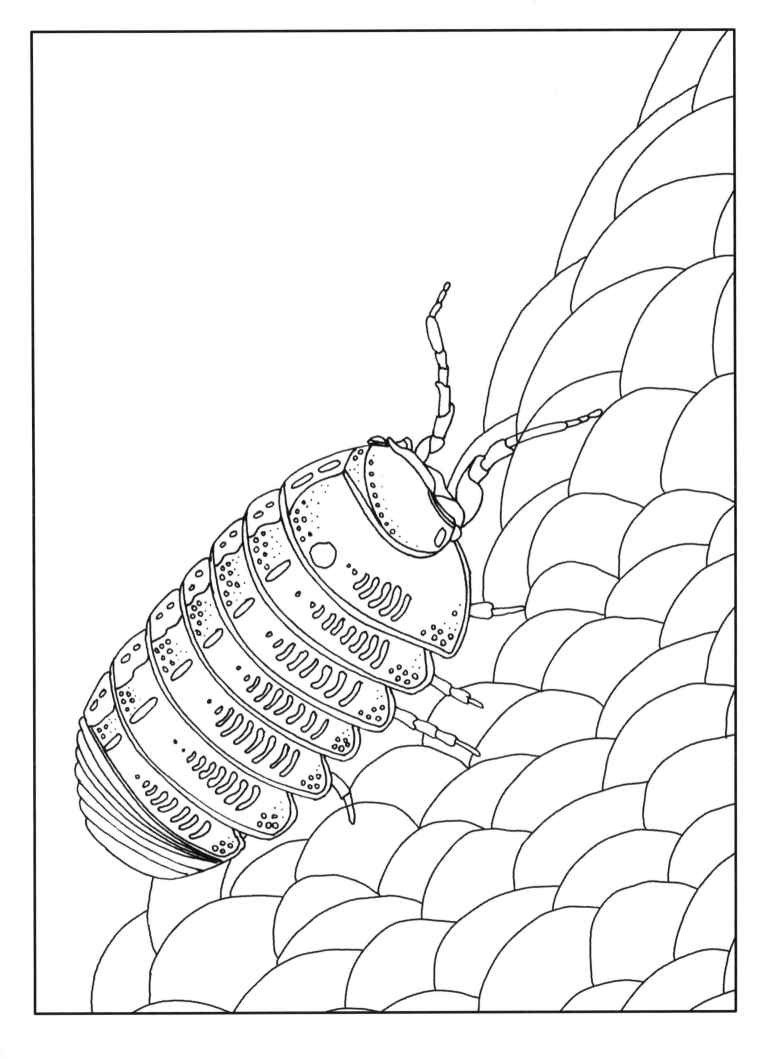

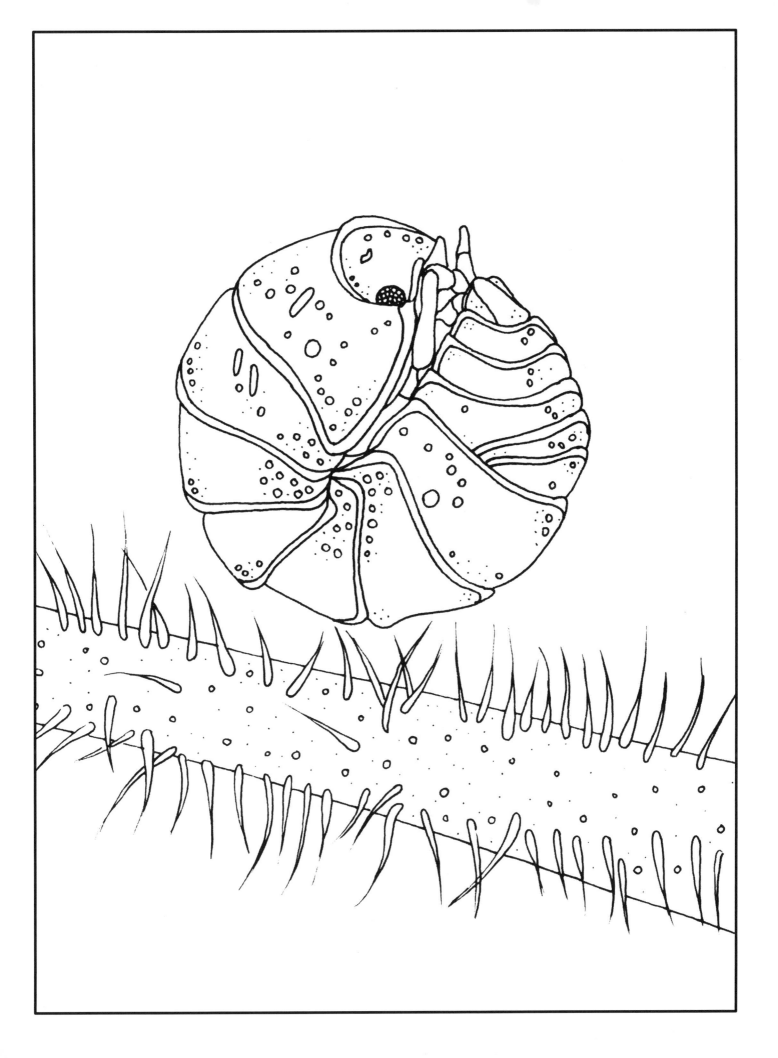

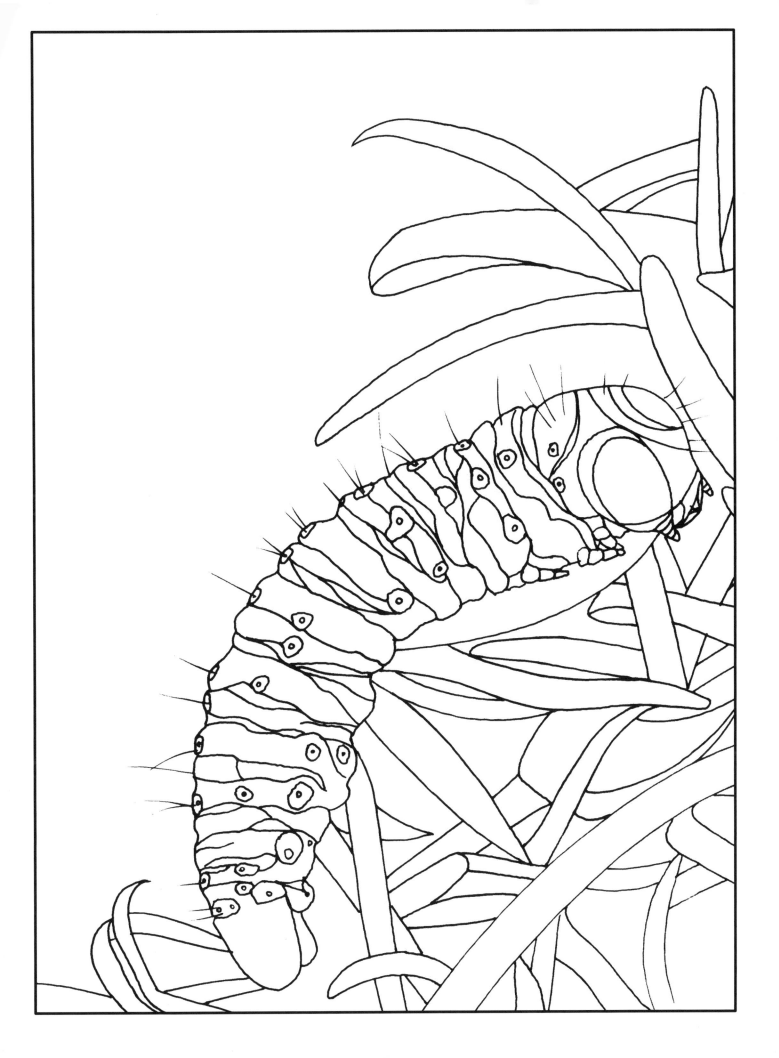

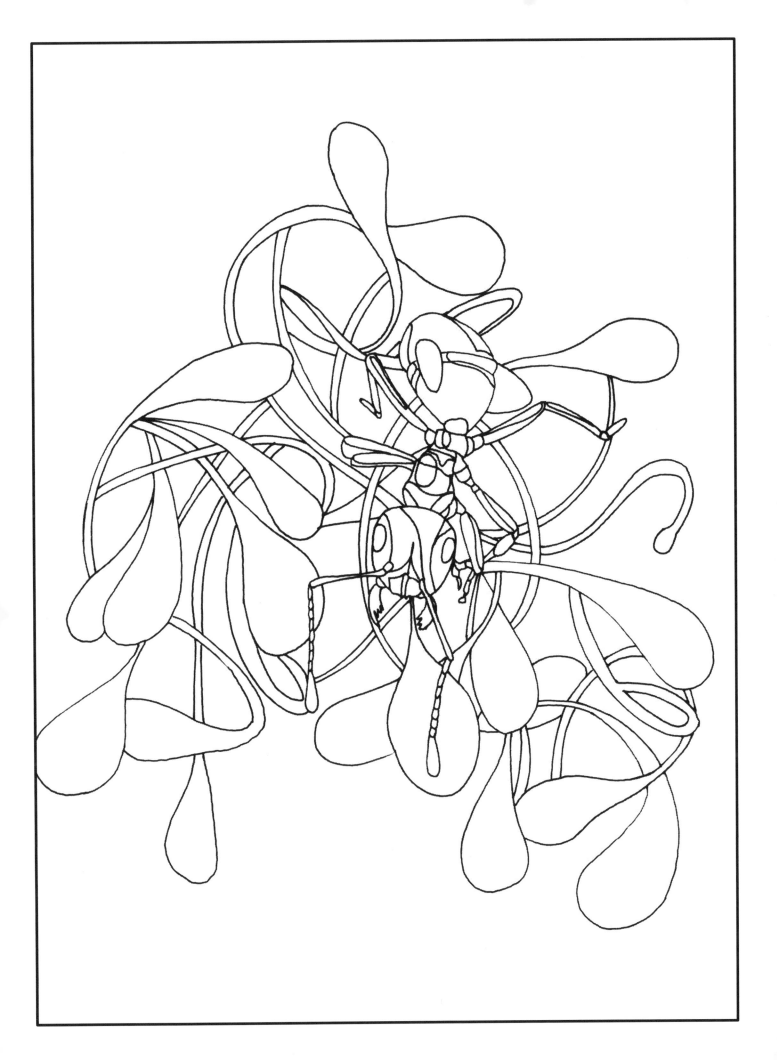

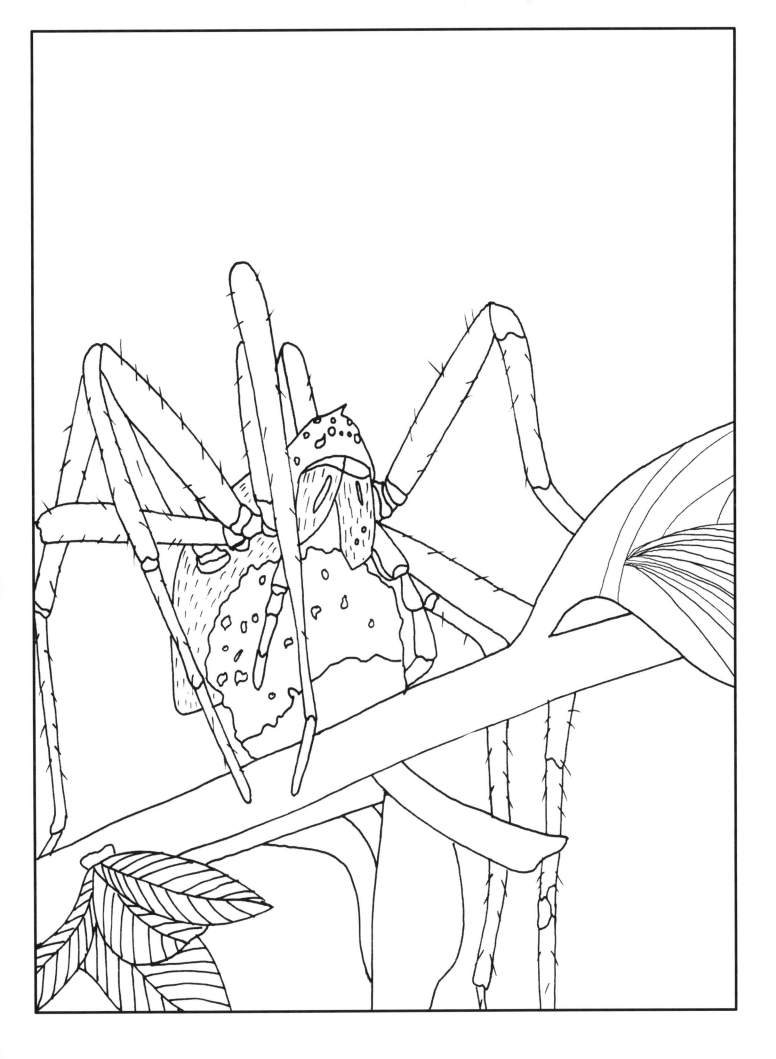

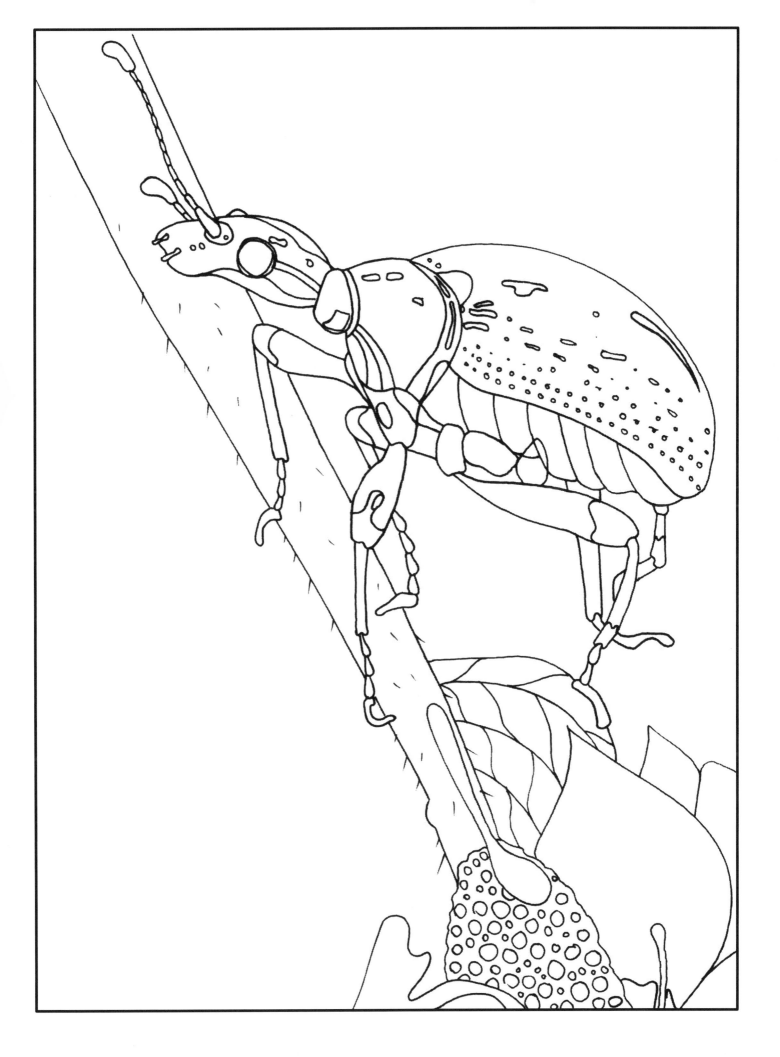

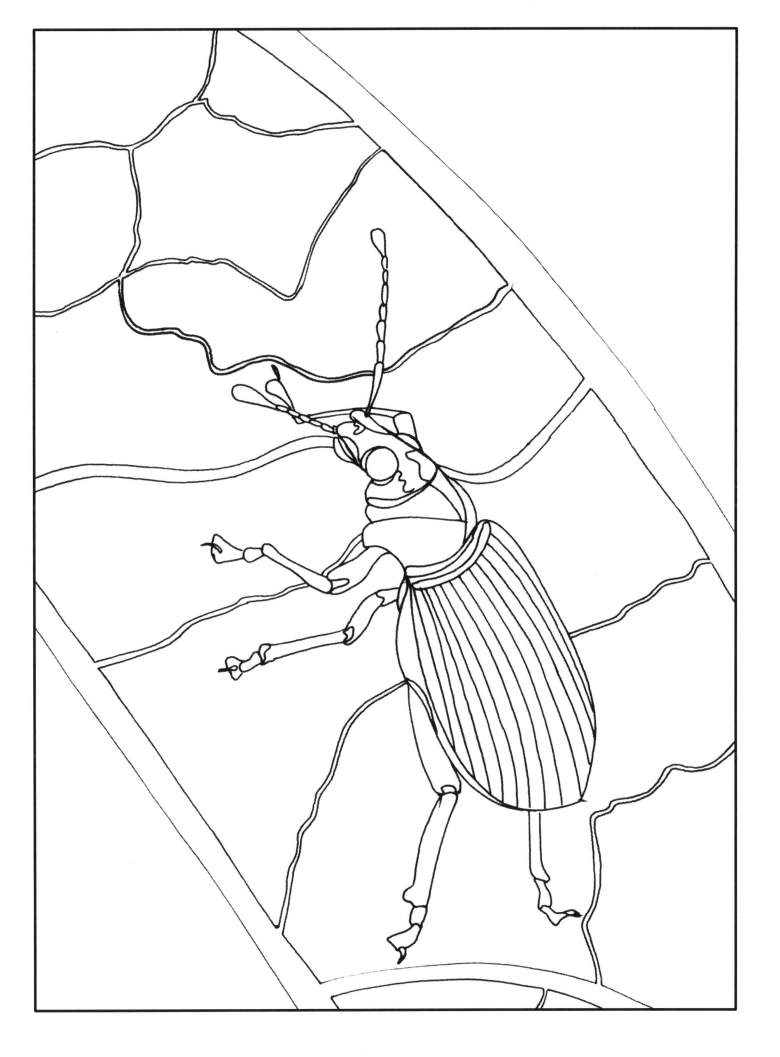

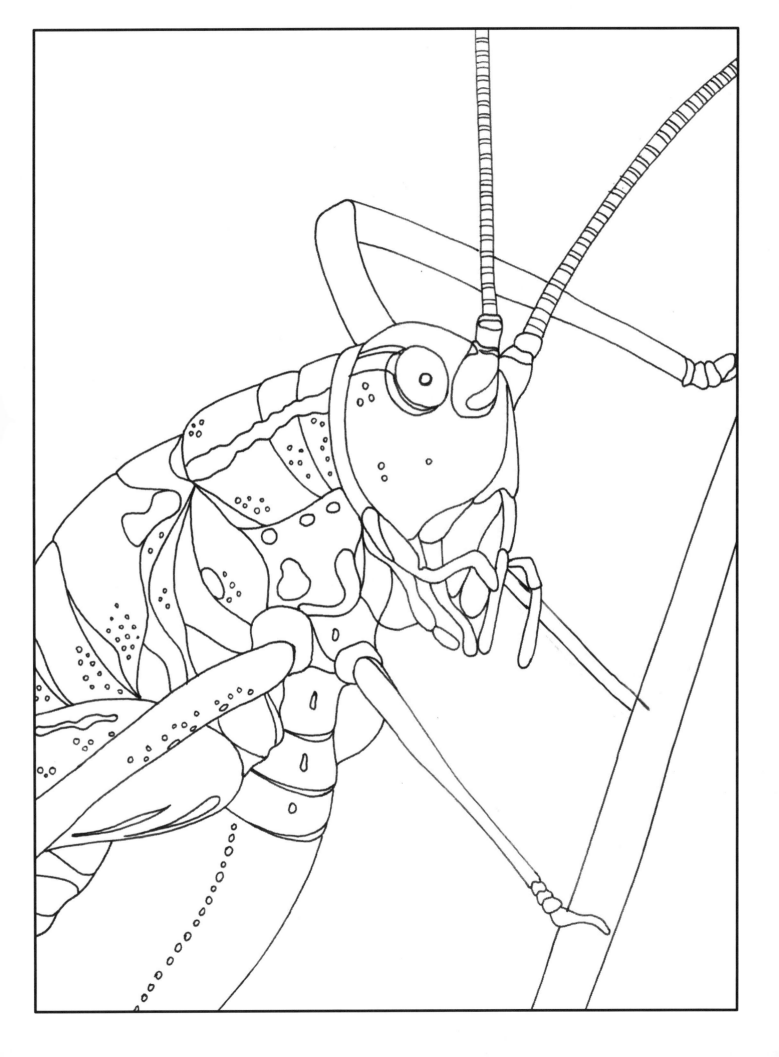

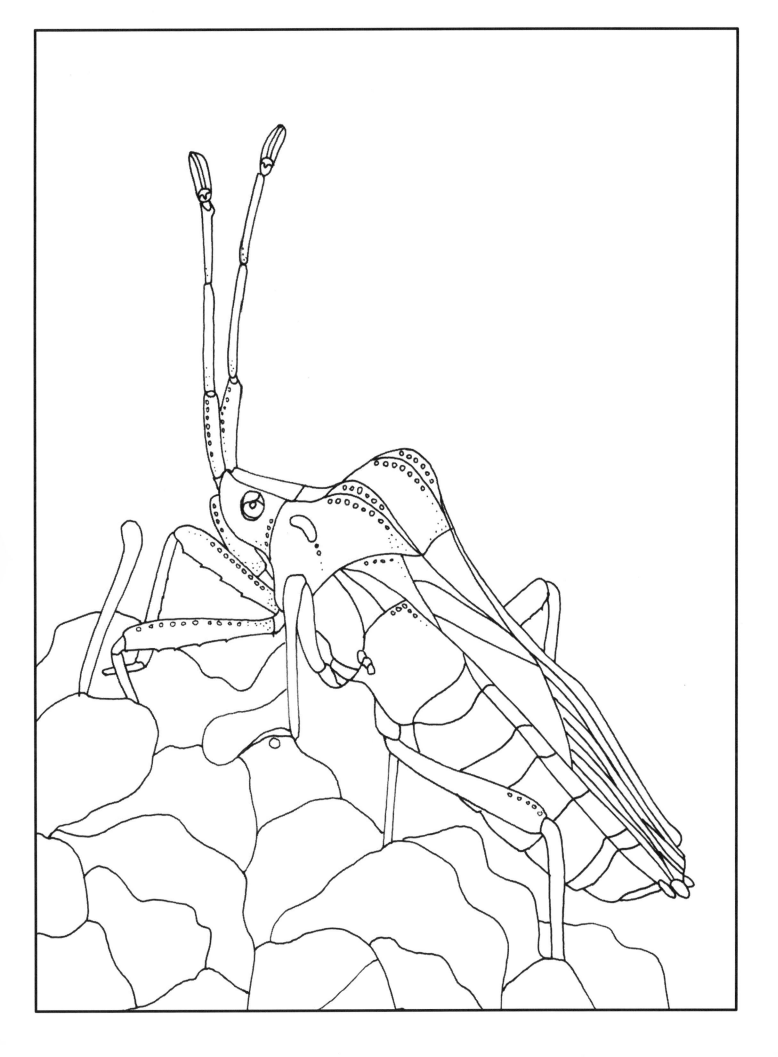

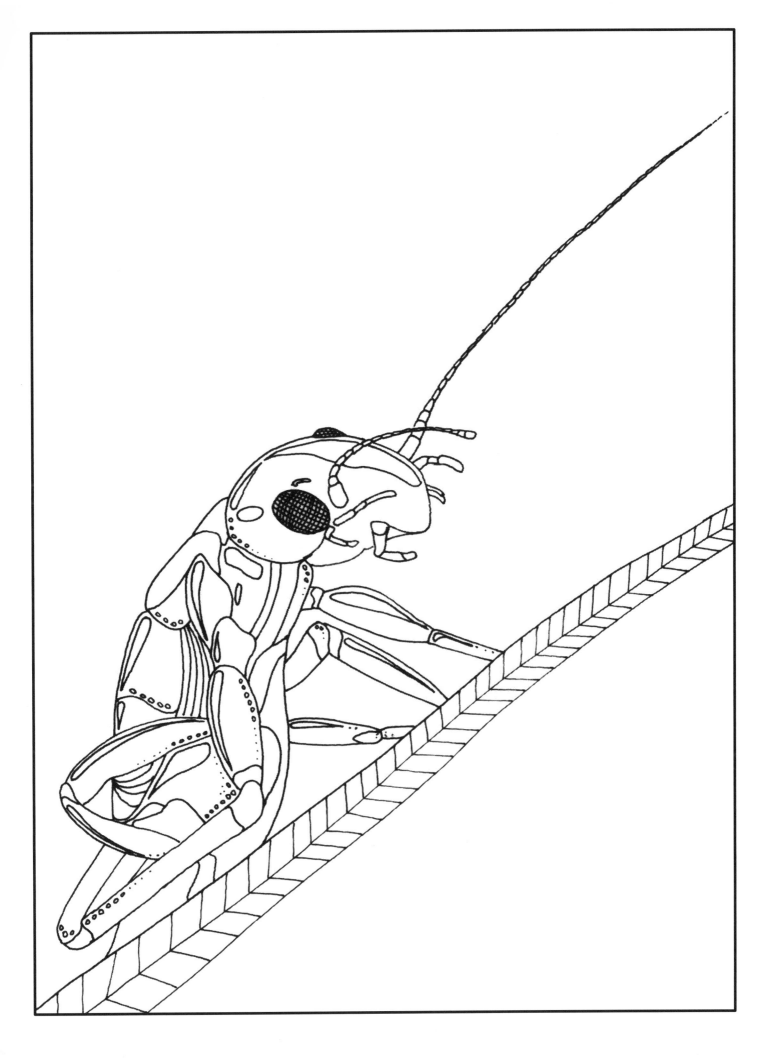

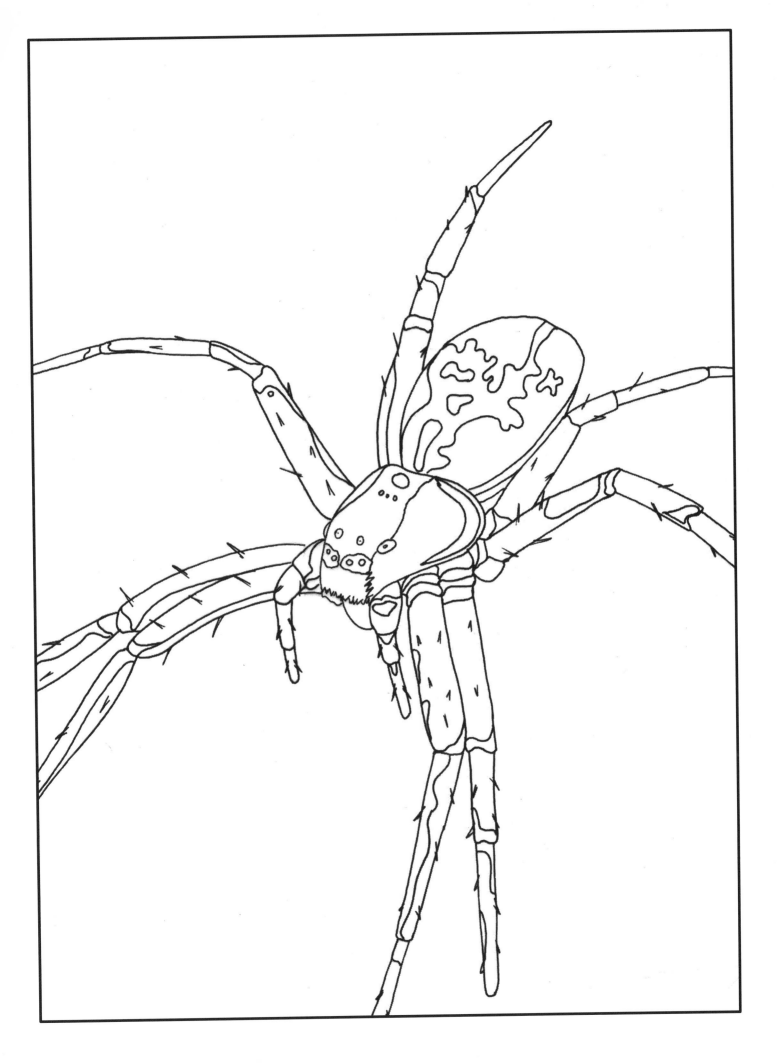

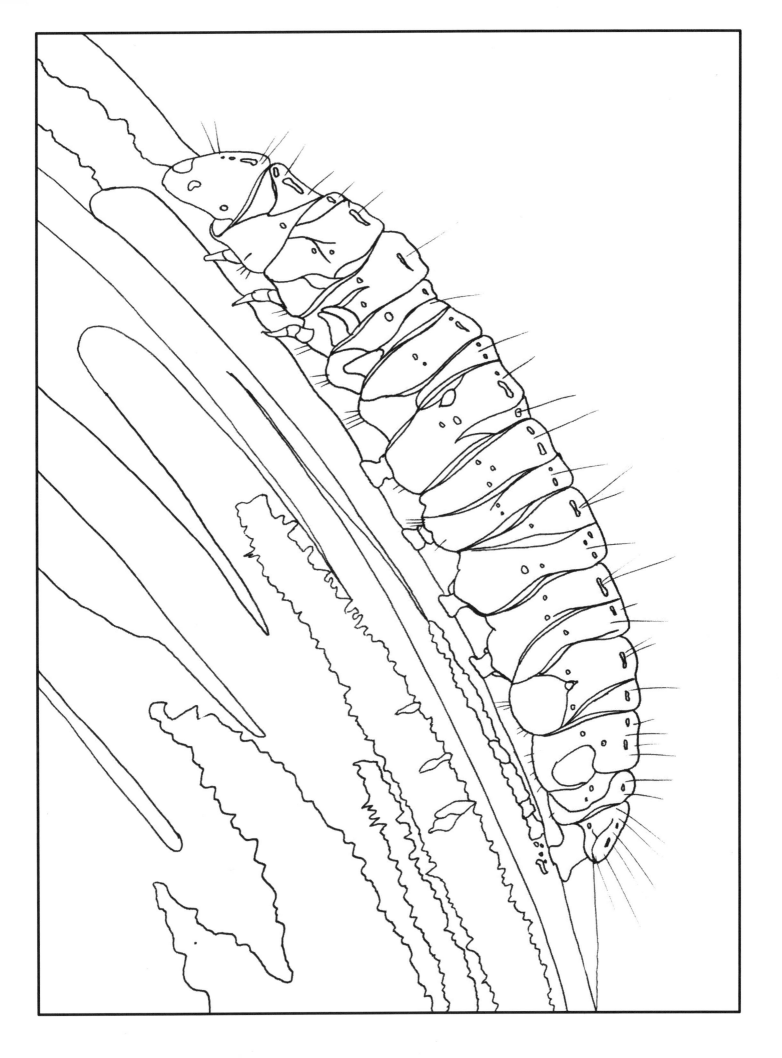

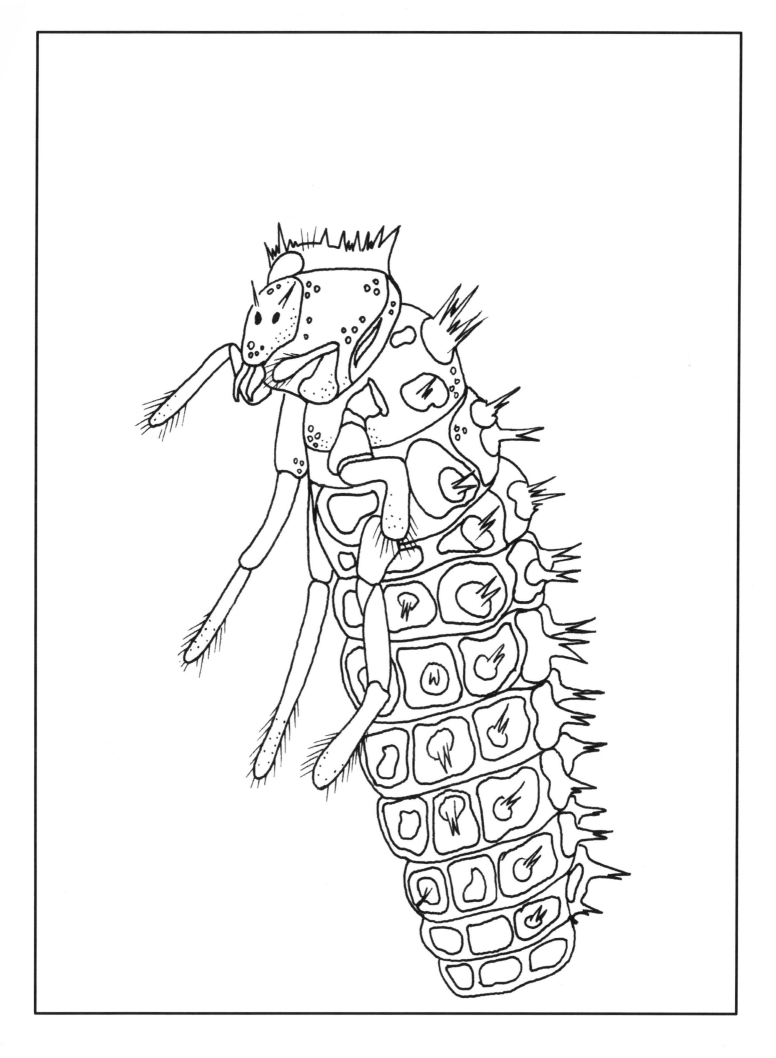

Why it is called Gizzy Books? My cat Gizzy was run over
by a car and I needed to raise money to pay for the vet bills.
She survived and she still occasionally bites my ears.

Published by Gizzy Books LTD 2016
Copyright © Nicholas Wright & Marta Rudyk

ISBN: 978-0-9955065-1-0

Like the book? Leave feedback on Amazon.
Every comment counts.

Made in the USA
Middletown, DE
24 December 2020